MY FAMILY REMEMBERS

The 1960s

Kath Walker

W
FRANKLIN WATTS
LONDON • SYDNEY

First published in 2011 by
Franklin Watts
338 Euston Road, London NW1 3BH

Franklin Watts Australia
Level 17/207 Kent Street, Sydney NSW 2000

© 2011 Franklin Watts

ISBN: 978 1 4451 0103 3

Dewey classification number: 941'.0856

A CIP catalogue record for this publication is available from the British Library.

Printed in China

Franklin Watts is a division of Hachette Children's Books, an Hachette UK Company.

www.hachette.co.uk

Planned and produced by Discovery Books Ltd., 2 College Street,
Ludlow, Shropshire, SY8 1AN
www.discoverybooks.net
Editor: James Nixon
Design: Blink Media

Photo credits: Flickr: p. 25 bottom (Tommy McClellan); Getty Images: pp. 13 top (John Pratt), 14 top, 16 top (SSPL), 18 bottom (Redferns), 19 top (Central Press), 20 top (Roy Jones), 21 top (Fred Mott); Mary Evans Picture Library: pp. 6 top (Ad Lib Studios), 7 right (Interfoto), 10, 12 top, 17 middle; NASA Kennedy Space Center: p. 7 left; Peter Spilsbury: p. 15 top; Rex Features: p. 15 bottom (Everett Collection); Russell Hobbs Limited: p. 12 bottom; Science and Society Picture Library: p. 28 top (National Railway Museum); Staffordshire Arts and Museum Service: p. 22 top; Suzanne Nixon: pp. 20 bottom, 25 top; Wikimedia: pp. 6 bottom (Adrian Pingstone), 17 top (Alex Kouprianov), 17 middle-right, 18 top (United Press International), 19 middle (Jorge Barrios), 21 bottom (Ed Yourdon); www.picturethepast.org: pp. 8 bottom (Courtesy of R Wilsher), 9 top (Courtesy of Nottinghamshire City Council), 9 middle (Courtesy of Copyright – Nottingham Evening Post), 11 top (Courtesy of W E Middleton & Son), 14 bottom (Courtesy of Nottinghamshire City Council), 23 top and middle (Courtesy of Buxton Museum and Art Gallery), 24 top (Courtesy of Derbyshire Libraries), 24 bottom (Courtesy of North Notts Newspapers Ltd), 25 middle (Courtesy of Derbyshire Libraries), 26 top (Courtesy of Nottinghamshire City Council), 26 bottom (Courtesy of Derbyshire Libraries), 27 top (Courtesy of L Clark), 27 bottom (Courtesy of Mr Bryn Roberts), 29 top (Courtesy of Derbyshire Libraries).

Cover photos: Wikimedia: left (United Press International); Mary Evans Picture Library: right.

Every attempt has been made to clear copyright. Should there be any inadvertent omission please apply to the publisher for rectification.

Words that are **bold** in the text are explained in the glossary.

Note to parents and teachers
Every effort has been made by the Publishers to ensure that the websites in this book are suitable for children, that they are of the highest educational value, and that they contain no inappropriate or offensive material. However, because of the nature of the Internet, it is impossible to guarantee that the contents of these sites will not be altered. We strongly advise that Internet access is supervised by a responsible adult.

Contents

4   Meet the families

6   Exciting changes

8   Places to live

10   Going shopping

12   Life at home

14   Film and television

16   Having fun

18   The decade of pop

20   Fashion

22   At work

24   Schooldays

26   Getting about

28   Holiday time

30   Find out what your family remembers

31   Glossary

32   Further information

32   Index

 Downloadable activity and information sheets are available at www.franklinwatts.co.uk

Meet the families

This book looks at life in the 1960s. The hard times of the '40s and '50s were over at last. Fast-changing styles in fashion and art brought colour into people's homes and lives – it seemed as if a new age had begun. Four children's families share their memories of those days.

Alice

Alice's family

Alice Hibberd is 13 years old. She has an older sister called Meg and lives with her mother, Julie, and stepfather, Tony. Tony, born in 1948, was in his teens and early twenties in the 1960s while Julie, born in 1959, was aged between 1 and 10. Alice's grandparents, Stan and June were born in the 1930s.

Tony

Julie

Stan

June

Sarah

Sarah's family

Sarah Hadland is 12 years old and lives with her older brother, Jacob, and parents, Marcia and Dan. Sarah's grandmother, Ruby, was born in Jamaica in 1937 and moved to the UK in the 1950s. She was in her twenties and early thirties during the '60s and got married in 1965.

Ruby

Matty

Hazel

Matty's family

Matty Morris is 12 years old and lives with his parents, Julie and Kevin. He has a younger sister called Milly and an older brother called Peter. His grandfather, Derek, was born in 1944 and his grandmother, Linda, was born in 1947. They were both in their teens and early twenties in the 1960s.

Hazel's family

Hazel Stancliffe is 11 years old. She lives with her older sister, Lily, and her parents, Abigail and Paul. Her grandmother, Jean, and step-grandfather, Adrian, were born in the 1940s and were both in their twenties during the 1960s. Adrian's younger brother, Rob, was born in 1953 and was aged between 7 and 16 in the '60s.

Derek

Linda

Jean

Adrian

Rob

Exciting changes

In the 1960s, people had more money to spend and more time to enjoy themselves than ever before. Big changes in fashion, music and ideas made it an exciting time, especially for young people.

This couple are posing in London's Carnaby Street, a centre for fashion in the 1960s.

There were major steps forward in science and technology. In 1961, Russian astronaut Yuri Gagarin became the first man into space and in 1969 American Neil Armstrong was the first man to walk on the Moon. Anything seemed possible.

'The new airliner Concorde flew for the first time at twice the speed of sound.'

Alice asks her stepfather about his memories of the 1960s:

In 1969, the new airliner Concorde flew for the first time at twice the speed of sound. I lived close to the airfield where it used to land. At my wedding, it flew over the village hall. All the guests rushed outside to look – right in the middle of my speech!

Concorde was the world's fastest passenger aircraft.

On 20 July 1969, the first humans landed on the Moon. In the background you can see their landing craft, *Eagle*.

A ship arrives in Southampton Harbour on 30 June 1962 bringing immigrants from the Caribbean.

Sarah asks her grandmother about life in the 1960s:

I lived and worked in Birmingham in the '60s and there was a lot of **racism** then. Some people treated me well, but others were very unpleasant. I used to get together with other Jamaicans and we'd go to each other's homes to listen to music, eat and play games. The neighbours used to report us to the police for causing trouble just because we were black.

There were plenty of jobs in Britain but not enough workers to do them. In the early '60s the government encouraged people from overseas to come to work in Britain. **Immigrants** arrived from the countries of the Caribbean, India and Pakistan. Unfortunately, many were treated badly and unfairly because of their race.

7

Places to live

Many people in the UK today own their homes. However, in the past more people rented houses or flats. Things started to change in the 1960s when more people could afford to buy their own homes.

The **population** of the UK was growing in the '60s and whole new towns were built.

This picture shows a new council estate in Chesterfield, Derbyshire, in 1962. People who needed homes could rent these houses at affordable prices.

Alice asks her stepfather about where he lived:
We lived in a **council house** until 1967, when my father bought a house on the other side of town. It cost him more than half his **wages** each month, but he was really proud to live in a home that he owned. My father was the first in his family to own his own home.

TIME DIFFERENCE

In 1961, nearly 43 per cent of homes were owned by the people living in them. By 1969, the figure had increased to 49 per cent. In 2010, about 67 per cent of homes were owned by those living in them.

Some older housing was in very bad condition. Local councils pulled down these **slums** and replaced them with new homes. In cities, these were often flats in high **tower blocks**.

Not everyone was happy to move into the new homes. Pulling down the old slums sometimes parted people from friends and family. Some of the tower blocks had been badly built and a few even became unsafe.

This photograph shows slums being cleared in the 1960s.

Tower blocks, like this one in Nottingham, provided many new homes in city areas.

Sarah asks her grandmother about the house she lived in:

In the early '60s, I rented a room in a house and shared a kitchen. Sometimes I would go to cook a meal only to find that someone had stolen my food. When I got married in 1965 (right), I was really happy to move into a house of our own.

'I was really happy to move into a house of our own.'

Going shopping

There were changes in the way that people shopped during the '60s. Most homes had fridges, so there was no need to buy fresh food every day. New supermarkets were opening around the country selling all types of food under one roof.

In parts of the country, old town centres were being knocked down or changed to make way for new shopping centres.

Supermarkets, like this Tesco's, were able to sell many foods at lower prices than the small local shops.

Hazel asks her great-uncle about the shops he used:

My mother would shop for food every day. A lot of our food came from local shops, and a lot of it was delivered to the house. But once every week or fortnight we'd catch a bus or walk to the supermarket which was about two miles [3.2 km] away.

TIME DIFFERENCE

In 1961, there were just 50 supermarkets in the UK. By 1969, the number had increased to 3,400. In 2009 there were 6,410 large supermarkets in the country.

Credit became a popular way of paying for expensive items, such as washing machines or television sets. In some stores, shoppers could spread payments over a couple of years. Smaller items, such as food or clothes, were usually paid for in cash. This was in pounds, shillings and pence, with 12 pence to a shilling and 20 shillings to a pound.

In the 1960s, supermarkets were built in town centres. Today, the bigger supermarkets are often in out-of-town locations.

Alice asks her grandmother what shopping was like:
We used to collect Green Shield stamps from shops and petrol stations. The more you spent, the more of these stamps you were given. We'd lick them and stick them into books. When we had collected enough, we could exchange the books for gifts such as electric toasters, towels and toys.

'We used to collect stamps from shops.'

Life at home

During the 1960s, many houses had gas or electric heating. This meant that homes became warmer. A few of the older houses still did not have indoor toilets, but almost all had electricity.

More people were able to afford electrical goods for the home and by the mid-1960s, 44 per cent of homes had a washing machine. In the kitchen, electric food mixers, toasters and kettles were making it quicker to prepare meals.

Twin-tub washing machines were popular in the '60s. Clothes were washed in one drum and spin dried in the other.

This Russell Hobbs electric kettle was the best-selling kettle in Britain during the 1960s. It switched itself off when the water boiled.

Matty asks his grandmother about her housework:
My first baby was born in the late '60s. In those days we didn't have nappies that you just threw away when they were dirty. Nappies were made of cloth and every day I had to wash and boil them. Then I put them through a **mangle** to wring out the water. I used to listen to music on the record player to make washing less boring.

'I used to listen to music on the record player.'

People decorated their homes with bright colours, bold patterns and white paintwork. A lot of furnishings were made of plastic or nylon and had smooth, modern shapes. In the late '60s, a softer look with Indian rugs and fabrics became fashionable.

Alice asks her stepfather about life at home:

In the '60s, we had a green fitted carpet put into the lounge. Wall-to-wall carpets were a new idea from America. It felt very snug not to have to put your feet down on to cold floor. We couldn't afford to have it in any other room though. We also had a telephone. This was good in some ways, but bad in others. The neighbours kept coming in to use it!

This 1960s telephone has a number dial instead of push-buttons. Unlike some phones we have today, '60s phones were not cordless.

Film and television

The number of people going to the cinema dropped during the 1960s as people stayed at home to watch television instead. Many of the big old cinemas closed down. However, **musicals** such as *Oliver!* and *The Sound of Music* were watched by big audiences. Spy movies were also very popular and in 1962 the first James Bond film was released.

A scene from the Bond movie *Thunderball,* with Sean Connery (left) playing the part of James Bond.

'I would rush to get front seats in the balcony.'

Hazel asks her great-uncle about going to the cinema:

I loved going to the old cinemas. My favourite was the Walpole in Ealing. It had a huge screen and could seat hundreds of people. My little brother and I would rush to get front seats in the balcony. Our mum took us to see the James Bond movies which we loved. Best of all we liked the fantastic cars he drove.

In the '60s, there were still some of the old cinemas left, like this one. Many others were pulled down or turned into bowling alleys or bingo halls.

14

TIME DIFFERENCE

In 1960, 510 million cinema tickets were sold in the UK. By 1969, the number had dropped to 215 million. In 2009, 174 million tickets were sold.

In 1964, television viewers got a new third channel, BBC2, to add to BBC1 and ITV. Then in 1967, BBC2 became the first channel to **broadcast** in colour. There were lots of new programmes for children. These included the cartoons *Huckleberry Hound* and *The Flintstones,* and puppet series *Stingray* and *Thunderbirds.* Some '60s shows, such as as *Dr Who* and *Coronation Street*, are still running today.

Here are some cinema tickets from the 1960s.

American cartoon series *The Flintstones* was set in the Stone Age town of Bedrock.

Alice asks her mother about children's TV programmes:
One of my favourite TV programmes was *Tales of the Riverbank*. It was stories about Hammy the Hamster who lived in an old boot and his animal friends. It showed film of real animals with human voices for the different characters.

Having fun

These are some of the top toys of the '60s. The doll on the bottom right is a Sindy.

In the 1960s, children had no electronic games or computers like today, but there were some fun new games and toys. Lots of girls had a Sindy or Barbie doll, and collected outfits in the latest fashions to dress them in. For boys, there were Action Man dolls that came with military uniforms and equipment.

Hazel asks her great-uncle about the games he played: I spent a lot of time playing cricket in the back garden (right) or playing war games with plastic model soldiers. My younger brother had a huge toy gun called a Johnny Gun that fired plastic bullets and rockets. If my mother was out, we'd take turns trying to shoot the plastic statue of a saint she kept on the stair post.

Hazel's great-uncle and his brother play with their guns in the back garden.

Other popular toys included Scalextric, Etch-a-Sketch, Spirograph and Meccano model kits. Some toys were linked to TV series or films, such as the model of the Aston Martin car from the James Bond movies. It had a flip-up roof and a special seat that could throw enemies out.

A Spirograph (top) and some of the amazing patterns that you could make with it.

Three young boys build a complicated vehicle with a Meccano set, a screwdriver and a spanner.

Alice asks her mother about her favourite toys:

When I was little, my favourite toys were a large donkey on wheels (pictured right) and a big teddy with a low growl. Then when I was a bit older, I had a model of the flying car from the film *Chitty Chitty Bang Bang* that I loved. It had wings that folded out.

The decade of pop

In 1963, a new sound hit the music scene. Liverpool band The Beatles had a huge success with *Please Please Me* and went on to have 17 number 1 hits in the UK. Screaming fans followed the band wherever they went and a new word was invented – 'Beatlemania'.

The Beatles arriving in the USA in 1964. From right to left: John, Paul, George and Ringo.

Hazel asks her step-grandfather about the music he liked:

I liked The Beatles a lot and went to one of their concerts in 1964. The music was great, but the screaming girls were awful. It made our ears hurt for the rest of the day.

'I liked The Beatles a lot, but the screaming girls were awful.'

The Beatles and many other British bands such as The Kinks and The Rolling Stones, were also very popular in the USA.

The Rolling Stones perform at a free concert in Hyde Park, London, in 1969.

In the late '60s, outdoor pop **festivals** were a new way of enjoying music in the summertime.

Transistor radio

At the beginning of the '60s there were no pop music radio stations in Britain. To listen to pop music, people could tune their small, battery-run **transistor radios** to Radio Luxembourg or **pirate radio stations**. Pirate stations broadcasted music from boats off the coast, but in 1967 a new law forced them to close down. That same year, the BBC launched its own pop station, Radio One.

Alice asks her stepfather how he listened to pop music:

I first heard The Beatles on Radio Luxembourg. The sound was not like anything I'd ever heard before. I bought every record The Beatles made. When I was 15, I joined a group as lead singer and we played at local village halls. We called ourselves The Captives.

Fashion

In the 1960s, London was a world fashion centre. **Boutiques** sprung up around the country selling colourful clothes for young people. In 1965, British designer Mary Quant launched the mini skirt for women.

There were also big changes in men's fashion. In the early '60s, a **trendy** suit had tight-fitting trousers, a collarless jacket and was worn with pointy boots.

The mini dresses that these girls are wearing were the height of fashion in 1968.

Narrow trousers and skinny ties were fashionable for men in the early '60s.

Matty asks his grandfather about the clothes he wore:

I used to go to dances in the nearby town dressed in tight-fitting drainpipe trousers and pointy 'winkle picker' shoes. These dances would often end in fighting between two groups – the mods and the rockers. The rockers wore black leather jackets and drove motorbikes. The mods rode scooters and liked dressing up in suits.

By the late '60s, men were wearing colourful clothes, sometimes made with velvet, satin or lace. Long hair, frilled or **paisley**-patterned shirts and flared trousers were in fashion.

Hazel asks her grandmother what clothes she wore:
Afghan coats made of sheepskin or goatskin were very fashionable in the late '60s. I had a goatskin one that was decorated with beautiful embroidery. The coat wasn't very good in the rain though. When it got wet it smelt awful – like damp goat!

Long hair and paisley shirts, like this one, were fashionable for men in the late '60s.

'When it got wet it smelt awful – like damp goat!'

By the late '60s, lots of people were wearing **hippie** styles. Hippies were young people who believed in love and peace. They liked to wear loose, flowing clothes made of natural silk or cotton. Indian prints were popular and beads, bells and headbands were common accessories.

Patterned clothing and scarves tied around the head were part of the hippie style.

At work

In the 1960s, wages increased and working hours were shortened. There were lots of jobs, partly because people had more money to spend. More workers were needed to make the things that people wanted to buy.

Industries such as mining and shipbuilding were becoming less important, but there were still lots of factories and plenty of new jobs in **service industries.** These are industries or businesses that do not make goods. Instead they provide a service, such as teaching, entertainment or travel. By 1965, more than half of all British workers were employed in service industries.

A female worker operates some machinery in a shoe factory. In the 1960s Britain made more goods than it does today.

Matty asks his grandmother about her job:
Straight after I left school at 15 I joined WHSmith to work as a sales assistant. My manager was called Mr Gill. He used to give me a bonus every time I sold a boxed fountain pen.

Matty's grandmother at work in WHSmith in the early 1960s.

Alice asks her stepfather about working life:

I joined a bank in 1965, when I was 16. When I joined, women were treated very unfairly. They mainly worked as **cashiers** and were hardly ever given more senior jobs. After six months at the bank, the boys were sent on a six-week training course, but not the girls. And if a woman became pregnant, she lost her job!

An old-style bank of the 1960s. Banks did not have computers or cash machines.

At the start of the '60s, about one-third of the workers were women – fewer than today. They were paid less than men for doing the same work. Through the decade, many women fought hard for the right to be treated equally.

Matty asks his grandfather about the work he did:

I was a policeman in the '60s and the job was different in those days. We didn't have personal radios. When we were on foot patrol we had to go to a telephone box every hour in case the sergeant wanted to speak to us!

Matty's grandfather in police uniform (left) and one of his colleagues on a scooter (above).

Schooldays

In the 1960s, children had to go to school between the ages of 5 and 15. At age 11, all children sat the '11 Plus' exam. Those who passed went on to a grammar or technical school where they studied for further exams. Those who failed were sent to secondary modern schools. These concentrated on practical subjects, such as woodwork or cookery.

This primary school class photograph was taken in 1964.

A lot of people thought the '11 plus' exam was unfair. To give all children a better chance of a good education, the government introduced a single type of secondary school in 1965. This was called a **comprehensive school**.

Many new universities were built in the '60s. Grants were given to students so they had money to live on while they studied. This meant that more people from poorer families could afford to go to university.

An increase in the number of babies born meant that lots of new schools were built in the 1960s.

Sports day was an important event in the school calendar, just as it is today. Above is a certificate awarded for coming second place in the high jump. Below is a high jump competition in action.

Alice asks her stepfather about grammar schools:
I was at grammar school in the early '60s and most of the teachers were very strict. They wore black gowns. If you were badly behaved the teacher sometimes threw a wooden board rubber at you! This used to send up a cloud of dust.

'The teacher sometimes threw a wooden board rubber at you!'

Alice asks her mother about her schooldays:
I was at primary school in the '60s and I enjoyed my time there. We used to have free school milk, which came in small bottles and was delivered in crates. The crates were left in the schoolyard and in the summer it sometimes turned sour and tasted horrible from being left out in the heat.

A group of schoolchildren drink their free school milk from bottles.

Getting about

New roads and motorways were built to cope with the growing number of vehicles on the road. A top car of the 1960s was the small and stylish Mini, while many teenagers enjoyed zipping about on scooters.

The car at the front of this picture is a Mini. These small cars were ideal for driving around towns and cities.

Hazel asks her great-uncle how he travelled:

My parents didn't have a car and we mainly used buses and trains to get about. Our next-door neighbours had a car and were always happy to give us lifts. We were very excited when my brother came home from university with his first car, a Standard Eight (right).

This section of the M1 motorway was built in the 1960s. There was much less traffic than there is today.

Although there were fewer cars in the '60s than today, more people were dying in road accidents. New laws were passed to make travelling safer. From 1967, all new cars had to have safety belts in the front and a 70 mile an hour (113 kph) speed limit was put on motorways.

TIME DIFFERENCE

In 1966, there were 12 million vehicles on the road in the UK and 7,985 people were killed in accidents. In 2009, there were more than 34 million vehicles but only 2,222 road deaths.

There were big changes in railway travel. To cut costs, British Railways closed down more than 2,000 stations in towns and villages. These cuts were planned by Dr Richard Beeching and became known as 'Beeching Cuts'. Trains powered by **diesel** (right) or electricity replaced steam trains. The last steam service ran in 1968.

Trains like this diesel train replaced the old steam trains.

Alice asks her stepfather about the Beeching cuts:
The loss of so many railways in the 1960s was very sad. It was great having a train station or two in every town and lots of village stops too.

'The loss of so many railways was very sad.'

This 1967 photo shows a steam train arriving at Ambergate station for the very last time.

Holiday time

In the 1960s, most people took their holidays in the UK, but a growing number went abroad. Foreign travel was getting cheaper and **package tours** to Europe became popular. These were tours organised by travel companies.

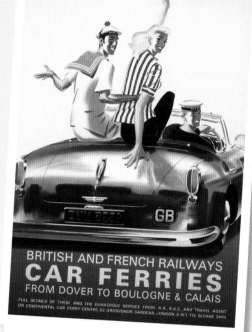

Cross with us to the Continent

BRITISH AND FRENCH RAILWAYS
CAR FERRIES
FROM DOVER TO BOULOGNE & CALAIS

FULL DETAILS OF THESE AND THE DUNKERQUE SERVICE FROM A.A., R.A.C. ANY TRAVEL AGENT OR CONTINENTAL CAR FERRY CENTRE, 52 GROSVENOR GARDENS, LONDON, S.W.1 TEL SLOANE 3440

Better roads and car ferry services meant that more people took motoring holidays in Europe.

A British family shop for souvenirs while on a package tour to Spain in the early '60s.

'We would travel by coach to a seaside resort.'

Sarah asks her grandmother if she went on holidays:
We didn't go on holidays during the 1960s but we sometimes went away on day trips. We would usually travel by coach to a seaside resort, such as Blackpool. I badly wanted to visit my old home in Jamaica but it cost too much. I couldn't afford to go there until 1975.

Many families who holidayed in the UK enjoyed going to holiday camps. At the camps they stayed in wooden chalets and could take part in lots of organised games and entertainment. A week at a holiday camp would cost a family about one week's wages.

Now that more people owned cars, many chose to go on camping or caravan holidays. Those who owned a caravan could tow it to a site of their choice. Others could rent one already in a caravan park. These parks were often near the sea and usually had their own shops and games rooms.

Lots of families spent holidays at caravan parks like this one.

Hazel asks her great-uncle where he went on holidays:

Each summer, my parents would rent a house in Sussex or Wales for two weeks. Dad would pay a driver from work to take us there. Our most exciting holiday was to the island of Guernsey in 1968 because we went by plane!

Rob and his younger brother on holiday at the British seaside.

Find out what your family remembers

Try asking members of your family what they remember about the 1960s. You could ask them the same questions that children in this book have asked and then compare the answers you get. Ask your relatives how they think that life in the '60s was different from today. Get them to talk about their favourite memories or important events of the time. This will help you build up your own picture of life in the 1960s. It will also help you find out more about your family history.

Timeline

1960 The first episode of *Coronation Street* is broadcast.

1961 Yuri Gagarin is the first astronaut in space.

1962 The first James Bond film *Dr No* is released. The Beatles have their first hit with *Love Me Do*.

1963 Dr Beeching makes huge cuts in the railway service.
US President John F Kennedy is assassinated.
First episode of *Dr Who* is broadcast.

1964 BBC 2 begins.

1965 Mary Quant introduces the mini skirt.

1966 England hosts and wins the World Cup.

1967 Television begins broadcasting in colour.
Pirate radio stations are closed down.
Radio One begins.
A new law is passed saying that all new cars must have safety belts in the front seats.

1968 The last steam passenger train runs in Britain.
Thousands gather in London's Grosvenor Square to **protest** against the Vietnam War.

1969 The USA lands the first man on the Moon.
Concorde makes its first supersonic flight.

Millennium 1999/27
World Cup/M White

26

This stamp, produced in 1999, shows England's football captain Bobby Moore holding the World Cup trophy in 1966.

Glossary

boutique
A small shop that specialises in selling goods such as clothes, gifts or jewellery.

broadcast
To send out by radio or television.

cashier
Someone who receives and pays out money at a bank or shop.

comprehensive school
A large secondary school for pupils of all abilities.

council house
A house controlled by a local council and rented out at a low rent.

credit
A system that allows someone to pay for an item over time.

diesel
A heavy oil used as fuel.

festival
A time of celebration, sometimes with entertainment and special events.

hippie
A person, or to do with people, who believed in love and peace, and behaved and dressed in a very relaxed and casual way.

immigrant
Someone who moves to another country, usually to live there permanently.

mangle
A machine operated by turning a handle that wrings the water out of wet washing.

musical
A film or play with lots of singing and dancing.

package tours
Tours organised by travel agents that include travel and accommodation in the price.

paisley
A swirly and colourful fabric design.

pirate radio station
A radio station that broadcasts without permission. In the 1960s, a few of these stations broadcast from ships.

population
All of the people living in a country or area.

protest
To do or say something to show that you object strongly.

racism
When people believe that some races are better than others and treat people of other races or colour badly.

renting
Paying money to live in a property that is owned by someone else.

service industry
An industry that supplies services such as entertainment, education, transport or healthcare, rather than goods.

slums
Homes that are in very poor condition and often overcrowded.

tower blocks
Tall buildings that are divided up into flats or offices.

transistor radio
A small radio that can be carried around.

trendy
In the latest fashion.

wages
The money paid to someone for the work they have done.

Further information

Books:
The 1960s (I Can Remember), Sally Hewitt, Franklin Watts, 2003
The 1960s: Age of Rock (20th Century Music), Heinemann Library, 2002
1960s The Satellite Age (20th Century Media), Steve Parker, Heinemann Library, 2003

Websites:
Watch some clips of children's TV shows of the 1960s on
http://www.wwwk.co.uk/television/childrens-tv/60s.htm
For a general outline of the 1960s with links to other websites, try
http://www.woodlands-junior.kent.sch.uk/homework/war/1960s.html
This BBC website has lots of memories from people who grew up in the 1960s
http://news.bbc.co.uk/1/hi/magazine/6707451.stm

Index

Beatles, The 18, 19, 30
Bond, James 14, 17, 30
boutiques 20, 31

caravans 29
carpets 13
cars 26, 29
cartoons 15
cinemas 14, 15
clothes 12, 20–21
comprehensive schools 24, 31
Concorde 6, 25, 30
council houses 8, 31

diesel 27, 31
dolls 16

electricity 12
exams 24

factories 22
fashion 4, 6, 16, 20–21, 31
festivals 19, 31
films 14–15, 17, 31
flats 8, 9, 31
fridges 10

grammar schools 24, 25

hippies 21, 31
holiday camps 29
holidays 28–29
houses 8, 9, 12, 31
housework 12

immigrants 7, 31
industries 22, 31

jobs 7, 22, 23

kettles 12

Mini 26
mini skirts 20, 30
motorways 26
musicals 14, 31

package tours 28, 31
paisley shirts 21
payments 11
pirate radio 19, 30, 31
pop music 18–19

racism 7, 31
radios 19, 31
railways 27, 30
record players 12, 13
Rolling Stones, The 18

schools 24–25, 31
shopping 10–11
shopping centres 10
slums 9, 31
steam trains 27, 30
suits 20
supermarkets 10, 11

telephones 13, 23
television 11, 14–15, 17, 30, 31
toys 16–17

universities 24

wages 8, 22, 29, 31
washing machines 11, 12
work 22–23
World Cup 30

Here are the lists of contents for each title in *My Family Remembers...*

1950s
Meet the families • After the war • Places to live • Going shopping • Life at home
Having fun • Television and film • Sounds of the '50s • Petticoats and Teddy Boys
Schooldays • At work • Getting about • Holiday time • A new beginning

1960s
Meet the families • Exciting changes • Places to live • Going shopping
Life at home • Film and television • Having fun • The decade of Pop
Fashion • At work • Schooldays • Getting about • Holiday time

1970s
Meet the families • Gloom and glitter • Life at home • Going shopping • Playtime
At the movies • Leisure time • From glam rock to punk • Fashions • Schooldays
At work • Getting about • Holiday time

1980s
Meet the families • A changing world • Life at home • Going shopping • Leisure time
Toys and crazes • Watching films • Sounds of the '80s • Power dressing to sportswear
Schooldays • At work • Getting about • Holiday time

1990s
Meet the families • The high-tech '90s • New technology • Going shopping
Leisure time • Video games and crazes • At the movies • Pop music
In fashion • Schooldays • At work • On the move • Going on holiday

2000s
Meet the families • The noughties • Technology at home • At work
Going shopping • Entertainment • Video gaming • On film • From CDs to iPods
In fashion • Schooldays • Travelling • Holidays